MAD LIBS

MAD SCIENTIST
MAD LIBS

concept created by Roger Price & Leonard Stern

PSS!

PRICE STERN SLOAN

An Imprint of Penguin Group (USA) LLC

PRICE STERN SLOAN
Published by the Penguin Group
Penguin Group (USA) LLC, 375 Hudson Street, New York, New York 10014, USA

USA | Canada | UK | Ireland | Australia | New Zealand | India | South Africa | China

penguin.com
A Penguin Random House Company

Published by Price Stern Sloan,
a division of Penguin Young Readers Group,
345 Hudson Street, New York, New York 10014.
Printed in the USA.

ISBN 978-0-8431-8057-2
1 3 5 7 9 10 8 6 4 2

MAD LIBS
INSTRUCTIONS

MAD LIBS® is a game for people who don't like games! It can be played by one, two, three, four, or forty.

• RIDICULOUSLY SIMPLE DIRECTIONS

In this tablet you will find stories containing blank spaces where words are left out. One player, the READER, selects one of these stories. The READER does not tell anyone what the story is about. Instead, he/she asks the other players, the WRITERS, to give him/her words. These words are used to fill in the blank spaces in the story.

• TO PLAY

The READER asks each WRITER in turn to call out a word—an adjective or a noun or whatever the space calls for—and uses them to fill in the blank spaces in the story. The result is a MAD LIBS® game.

When the READER then reads the completed MAD LIBS® game to the other players, they will discover that they have written a story that is fantastic, screamingly funny, shocking, silly, crazy, or just plain dumb—depending upon which words each WRITER called out.

• EXAMPLE (*Before* and *After*)

"_____!" he said _____
    EXCLAMATION   ADVERB

as he jumped into his convertible _____ and
                                          NOUN

drove off with his _____ wife.
                   ADJECTIVE

"*Ouch*!" he said *stupidly*
    EXCLAMATION   ADVERB

as he jumped into his convertible *cat* and
                                          NOUN

drove off with his *brave* wife.
                   ADJECTIVE

MAD ☺ IBS
QUICK REVIEW

In case you have forgotten what adjectives, adverbs, nouns, and verbs are, here is a quick review:

An ADJECTIVE describes something or somebody. *Lumpy, soft, ugly, messy,* and *short* are adjectives.

An ADVERB tells how something is done. It modifies a verb and usually ends in "ly." *Modestly, stupidly, greedily,* and *carefully* are adverbs.

A NOUN is the name of a person, place, or thing. *Sidewalk, umbrella, bridle, bathtub,* and *nose* are nouns.

A VERB is an action word. *Run, pitch, jump,* and *swim* are verbs. Put the verbs in past tense if the directions say PAST TENSE. *Ran, pitched, jumped,* and *swam* are verbs in the past tense.

When we ask for A PLACE, we mean any sort of place: a country or city (*Spain, Cleveland*) or a room (*bathroom, kitchen*).

An EXCLAMATION or SILLY WORD is any sort of funny sound, gasp, grunt, or outcry, like *Wow!, Ouch!, Whomp!, Ick!,* and *Gadzooks!*

When we ask for specific words, like a NUMBER, a COLOR, an ANIMAL, or a PART OF THE BODY, we mean a word that is one of those things, like *seven, blue, horse,* or *head.*

When we ask for a PLURAL, it means more than one. For example, *cat* pluralized is *cats.*

MAD LIBS® is fun to play with friends, but you can also play it by yourself! To begin with, DO NOT look at the story on the page below. Fill in the blanks on this page with the words called for. Then, using the words you have selected, fill in the blank spaces in the story.

Now you've created your own hilarious MAD LIBS® game!

HOW TO GET MY LOOK BY ALBERT EINSTEIN

OCCUPATION _____

ADVERB _____

ADJECTIVE _____

NOUN _____

ADJECTIVE _____

ADJECTIVE _____

COLOR _____

ADJECTIVE _____

PART OF THE BODY _____

NOUN _____

ARTICLE OF CLOTHING _____

OCCUPATION _____

MAD LIBS®

HOW TO GET MY LOOK
BY ALBERT EINSTEIN

Hallo. I am famous German _____ Albert Einstein. Some
OCCUPATION

people say I look _____ insane. And zey are right, I do! But
ADVERB

I am not actually _____. Zis is just how I like to look. If you
ADJECTIVE

would also like to look like zis, use ze makeover tips I have outlined

below.

- Never comb your _____: It is supposed to look like zis!
NOUN

The more _____, the better, as I always say. It also helps
ADJECTIVE

if your hair is a/an _____ shade of _____.
ADJECTIVE   COLOR

- Make _____ faces as often as possible. For example, stick
ADJECTIVE

out your _____ in pictures. Why? Because life is fun! Do
PART OF THE BODY

zis when your eager _____ students photograph you. Zey
NOUN

will love it!

- Always wear a white lab _____. Zis way, you
ARTICLE OF CLOTHING

will look like a real _____.
OCCUPATION

MAD LIBS® is fun to play with friends, but you can also play it by yourself! To begin with, DO NOT look at the story on the page below. Fill in the blanks on this page with the words called for. Then, using the words you have selected, fill in the blank spaces in the story.

Now you've created your own hilarious MAD LIBS® game!

THE BIOGRAPHY OF ALBERT EINSTEIN

A PLACE _____

NUMBER _____

OCCUPATION _____

ADJECTIVE _____

COLOR _____

ADJECTIVE _____

ADVERB _____

ADVERB _____

PLURAL NOUN _____

PLURAL NOUN _____

VERB (PAST TENSE) _____

NOUN _____

NOUN _____

NOUN _____

PART OF THE BODY _____

A PLACE _____

MAD LIBS

THE BIOGRAPHY OF ALBERT EINSTEIN

Albert Einstein was born in (the) _____ in Germany in the
_____ A PLACE

year 18-_____. He grew up to be a genius _____ with
_____ NUMBER _____ OCCUPATION

a/an _____ _____ head of hair and a/an
_____ ADJECTIVE _____ COLOR

_____ sense of humor. Even though he was _____
_____ ADJECTIVE _____ ADVERB

smart, the people who knew him thought he acted pretty

_____. He was notorious for losing _____ and
_____ ADVERB _____ PLURAL NOUN

forgetting the _____ in his equations. Einstein became
_____ PLURAL NOUN

famous for inventing things like E equals MC _____,
_____ VERB (PAST TENSE)

the theory of _____, and the quantum _____ of
_____ NOUN _____ NOUN

light. In 1921, he won the Nobel _____ in Physics. After his
_____ NOUN

death in 1955, Einstein's _____ was donated to (the)
_____ PART OF THE BODY

_____ Medical Center.
_____ A PLACE

From MAD SCIENTIST MAD LIBS® • Copyright © 2014 by Price Stern Sloan,
an imprint of Penguin Group (USA) LLC, 345 Hudson Street, New York, NY 10014.

MAD LIBS® is fun to play with friends, but you can also play it by yourself! To begin with, DO NOT look at the story on the page below. Fill in the blanks on this page with the words called for. Then, using the words you have selected, fill in the blank spaces in the story.

Now you've created your own hilarious MAD LIBS® game!

QUIZ: ARE YOU A MAD SCIENTIST?

ADJECTIVE _____

ADJECTIVE _____

EXCLAMATION _____

ADJECTIVE _____

ADJECTIVE _____

VERB (PAST TENSE) _____

TYPE OF LIQUID _____

ANIMAL (PLURAL) _____

COLOR _____

ADJECTIVE _____

NOUN _____

NOUN _____

ADJECTIVE _____

ARTICLE OF CLOTHING _____

ADJECTIVE _____

OCCUPATION _____

MAD LIBS
QUIZ: ARE YOU A
MAD SCIENTIST?

Are you crazy about science? Do you go nuts for _____
                                                    ADJECTIVE

experiments? Take this _____ quiz to find out if you're a mad
                          ADJECTIVE

scientist.

1. Your favorite saying is: a) "Oh, _____! What did I do?",
                                          EXCLAMATION

    b) "It's _____!", c) "This _____ experiment
                ADJECTIVE   ADJECTIVE

    went exactly as _____."
                       VERB (PAST TENSE)

2. Your lab always contains: a) test tubes filled with _____,
                                                            TYPE OF LIQUID

    b) _____ floating in jars, c) a few _____
          ANIMAL (PLURAL)   COLOR

    mice in cages.

3. Your favorite thing to do at night is: a) go to bed and have

    _____ dreams, b) laugh maniacally while bringing to life
       ADJECTIVE

    an evil _____, c) plan tomorrow's _____-work.
                NOUN   NOUN

If you answered mostly *B*s, guess what? You're a/an _____
                                                         ADJECTIVE

scientist! Go put on your long white _____ and
                                        ARTICLE OF CLOTHING

experiment in your _____ laboratory. If you answered mostly
                      ADJECTIVE

*A*s and *C*s, you're better off as a/an _____!
                                            OCCUPATION

MAD LIBS® is fun to play with friends, but you can also play it by yourself! To begin with, DO NOT look at the story on the page below. Fill in the blanks on this page with the words called for. Then, using the words you have selected, fill in the blank spaces in the story.

Now you've created your own hilarious MAD LIBS® game!

LAB RAT ON THE LOOSE

SILLY WORD _____

ADJECTIVE _____

NUMBER _____

NOUN _____

VERB ENDING IN "ING" _____

NOUN _____

TYPE OF LIQUID _____

ADJECTIVE _____

PART OF THE BODY _____

ADJECTIVE _____

VERB ENDING IN "ING" _____

ADJECTIVE _____

ANIMAL _____

ADJECTIVE _____

MAD LIBS

LAB RAT ON THE LOOSE

Uh-oh! Last night, _____ the lab rat escaped from his cage
                        SILLY WORD

and ran amok in the science lab. He was out to get revenge on the

_____ scientists who'd held him captive for _____
ADJECTIVE   NUMBER

weeks. First, he ran straight to the _____ tubes and knocked
                                      NOUN

them over, _____ glass all over the _____.
           VERB ENDING IN "ING"   NOUN

Then he jumped into a vat of _____ and left
                             TYPE OF LIQUID

_____ _____-prints all over the floor. Later on, the
ADJECTIVE   PART OF THE BODY

_____ rat finally got tired of _____ around
ADJECTIVE   VERB ENDING IN "ING"

and went to sleep under a/an _____-scope. Looks like that
                             ADJECTIVE

silly _____ is finally done with all his _____ hijinks.
      ANIMAL   ADJECTIVE

For now, at least . . .

MAD LIBS® is fun to play with friends, but you can also play it by yourself! To begin with, DO NOT look at the story on the page below. Fill in the blanks on this page with the words called for. Then, using the words you have selected, fill in the blank spaces in the story.

Now you've created your own hilarious MAD LIBS® game!

THE STORY OF FRANKENSTEIN

PERSON IN ROOM (MALE) _____

ADJECTIVE _____

NOUN _____

NOUN _____

A PLACE _____

PART OF THE BODY (PLURAL) _____

NUMBER _____

PLURAL NOUN _____

NOUN _____

ADJECTIVE _____

NOUN _____

ADJECTIVE _____

A PLACE _____

NOUN _____

NOUN _____

ADVERB _____

VERB (PAST TENSE) _____

MAD LIBS
THE STORY OF FRANKENSTEIN

Mary Shelley wrote a science-fiction book about a villainous mad

scientist called _____ Frankenstein. Frankenstein was
　　　　　　　　　　 PERSON IN ROOM (MALE)

a/an _____ scientist from the nineteenth _____. His
　　　 ADJECTIVE 　　　　　　　　　　　　　　　　　　 NOUN

greatest wish was to one day become a real _____. So he went
　　　　　　　　　　　　　　　　　　　　　　　　 NOUN

to (the) _____ and took a brain, some _____,
　　　　　 A PLACE 　　　　　　　　　　　 PART OF THE BODY (PLURAL)

and _____ legs from several dead _____. Once he
　　 NUMBER 　　　　　　　　　　　　 PLURAL NOUN

had sewn the body parts together, Frankenstein used electricity to

make the hideous _____ come to life. Soon, in the middle of
　　　　　　　　　 NOUN

a/an _____ and stormy _____, the creature awoke!
　　　 ADJECTIVE 　　　　　　　　 NOUN

It was Frankenstein's greatest creation, and one of the most

_____ beings to ever live—until it started terrorizing the
　　ADJECTIVE

citizens of (the) _____. Frankenstein had to take action. He
　　　　　　　　　 A PLACE

armed himself with a/an _____ and went on a hunt for the
　　　　　　　　　　　　　 NOUN

_____ he'd created. After searching _____ for
　　NOUN 　　　　　　　　　　　　　　　　　 ADVERB

months, Frankenstein finally had to give up his search because he

_____ .
　　VERB (PAST TENSE)

From MAD SCIENTIST MAD LIBS® • Copyright © 2014 by Price Stern Sloan,
an imprint of Penguin Group (USA) LLC, 345 Hudson Street, New York, NY 10014.

MAD LIBS® is fun to play with friends, but you can also play it by yourself! To begin with, DO NOT look at the story on the page below. Fill in the blanks on this page with the words called for. Then, using the words you have selected, fill in the blank spaces in the story.

Now you've created your own hilarious MAD LIBS® game!

ANNOUNCEMENT: THE SCIENCE FAIR WINNERS

CITY _____

ADVERB _____

ADJECTIVE _____

PERSON IN ROOM (FEMALE) _____

NOUN _____

SILLY WORD _____

PERSON IN ROOM (MALE) _____

ADJECTIVE _____

VERB (PAST TENSE) _____

PERSON IN ROOM _____

VERB ENDING IN "ING" _____

NUMBER _____

COLOR _____

ADJECTIVE _____

NOUN _____

ADJECTIVE _____

MAD LIBS
ANNOUNCEMENT: THE
SCIENCE FAIR WINNERS

Thank you all for participating in the _____ Middle School
<small>CITY</small>

Science Fair. Everyone worked very _____ on their projects
<small>ADVERB</small>

and it shows. We will now announce the first-, second-, and

_____-place winners.
<small>ADJECTIVE</small>

_____ won first prize for her miniature erupting
<small>PERSON IN ROOM (FEMALE)</small>

_____, which was a model of the largest volcano in history,
<small>NOUN</small>

Mount _____.
<small>SILLY WORD</small>

_____ got second place for his super _____
<small>PERSON IN ROOM (MALE)</small>   <small>ADJECTIVE</small>

miniature solar system, in which all the planets _____
<small>VERB (PAST TENSE)</small>

in circles.

_____ was given a third-place ribbon for _____
<small>PERSON IN ROOM</small>   <small>VERB ENDING IN "ING"</small>

an ant farm using sand and _____ tiny _____ ants.
<small>NUMBER</small>   <small>COLOR</small>

That's it for the _____ annual science fair. We'll see you next
<small>ADJECTIVE</small>

_____ for another round of _____ science
<small>NOUN</small>   <small>ADJECTIVE</small>

experiments.

MAD LIBS® is fun to play with friends, but you can also play it by yourself! To begin with, DO NOT look at the story on the page below. Fill in the blanks on this page with the words called for. Then, using the words you have selected, fill in the blank spaces in the story.

Now you've created your own hilarious MAD LIBS® game!

THE PERIODIC TABLE

PLURAL NOUN _____

NOUN _____

NOUN _____

ADJECTIVE _____

A PLACE _____

LAST NAME _____

PLURAL NOUN _____

NUMBER _____

NOUN _____

PLURAL NOUN _____

NOUN _____

LETTER OF THE ALPHABET _____

LETTER OF THE ALPHABET _____

PLURAL NOUN _____

VERB _____

MAD LIBS®
THE PERIODIC TABLE

The periodic table of _____ hangs in classrooms and
                          PLURAL NOUN

_____ laboratories all around the _____. So what's
   NOUN   NOUN

this _____ chart all about? Well, in the eighteenth
        ADJECTIVE

century, a chemist from (the) _____ named Dmitry
                                  A PLACE

_____ created the very first periodic table of
   LAST NAME

_____. There are more than _____ elements on the
 PLURAL NOUN   NUMBER

periodic table, organized by atomic _____. The elements all
                                          NOUN

have a certain number of protons, neutrons, and _____.
                                                    PLURAL NOUN

Each element on the periodic _____ has a symbol that is often
                                  NOUN

the first two letters of the element's name. For example, helium's

symbol is _____ _____. Some scientists
           LETTER OF THE ALPHABET   LETTER OF THE ALPHABET

say more _____ should be added to the table. Maybe
            PLURAL NOUN

someday you'll _____ one yourself!
                    VERB

From MAD SCIENTIST MAD LIBS® • Copyright © 2014 by Price Stern Sloan,
an imprint of Penguin Group (USA) LLC, 345 Hudson Street, New York, NY 10014.

MAD LIBS® is fun to play with friends, but you can also play it by yourself! To begin with, DO NOT look at the story on the page below. Fill in the blanks on this page with the words called for. Then, using the words you have selected, fill in the blank spaces in the story.

Now you've created your own hilarious MAD LIBS® game!

DR. JEKYLL AND MR. HYDE

OCCUPATION _____

CITY _____

NOUN _____

ADJECTIVE _____

PLURAL NOUN _____

VERB (PAST TENSE) _____

ADJECTIVE _____

ADVERB _____

VERB _____

PLURAL NOUN _____

ADJECTIVE _____

OCCUPATION _____

NOUN _____

NOUN _____

ADJECTIVE _____

NOUN _____

ADJECTIVE _____

TYPE OF LIQUID _____

PART OF THE BODY _____

MAD LIBS

DR. JEKYLL AND MR. HYDE

Dr. Jekyll was a friendly old _____ living in _____,
                                    OCCUPATION   CITY

England. Mr. Hyde was an evil young _____ who did
                                                        NOUN

_____ things to every person he met. But these two
ADJECTIVE

_____ were also a lot alike. They even kind of
PLURAL NOUN

_____ the same! But Hyde had a/an _____
VERB (PAST TENSE)   ADJECTIVE

power over the doctor, and became _____ evil as time went
                                          ADVERB

on. He was willing to _____ anyone who got in his way, and
                            VERB

even took _____ from the _____ townspeople.
                PLURAL NOUN   ADJECTIVE

Then Hyde murdered a well-known _____! But, what a
                                        OCCUPATION

surprise—it wasn't Hyde after all. It was Jekyll! They were the same

exact _____. Turns out, Jekyll had split-_____
          NOUN   NOUN

disorder. To fix this, Jekyll did _____ experiments on himself
                                        ADJECTIVE

so that Hyde would leave his _____ once and for all. But the
                                    NOUN

experiments were too _____. The chemicals and
                            ADJECTIVE

_____ didn't work. In the end, Hyde took over Jekyll's
TYPE OF LIQUID

_____, and Jekyll was never seen again.
PART OF THE BODY

From MAD SCIENTIST MAD LIBS® • Copyright © 2014 by Price Stern Sloan,
an imprint of Penguin Group (USA) LLC, 345 Hudson Street, New York, NY 10014.

MAD LIBS® is fun to play with friends, but you can also play it by yourself! To begin with, DO NOT look at the story on the page below. Fill in the blanks on this page with the words called for. Then, using the words you have selected, fill in the blank spaces in the story.

Now you've created your own hilarious MAD LIBS® game!

LABORATORY SAFETY DOS AND DON'TS

PART OF THE BODY (PLURAL) _____

NOUN _____

ADVERB _____

VERB ENDING IN "ING" _____

NOUN _____

VERB _____

ADJECTIVE _____

PART OF THE BODY (PLURAL) _____

TYPE OF FOOD _____

ADJECTIVE _____

TYPE OF CONTAINER _____

ANIMAL (PLURAL) _____

Do wear safety goggles. They will protect your _____.
PART OF THE BODY (PLURAL)

Don't light anything on fire. Always keep a/an _____
NOUN

extinguisher handy in case you _____ set your laboratory
ADVERB

aflame. **Do** clean the lens of the microscope before

_____ it. You might think you're looking at a cell
VERB ENDING IN "ING"

when really you're just looking at piece of _____. **Don't** get
NOUN

too close to the test tubes after combining their contents. They might

_____ all over you! **Do** clean up after yourself. Experiments
VERB

can leave you with _____ hands and stinky
ADJECTIVE

_____. **Don't** leave any experiments unattended. If
PART OF THE BODY (PLURAL)

you get hungry and want to grab a/an _____ sandwich, stop!
TYPE OF FOOD

You need to stay put until the _____ chemicals in your beakers
ADJECTIVE

are done boiling and you've put them safely away in a/an

_____. **Do** remember to feed your lab
TYPE OF CONTAINER

_____. They're not only your test subjects, they're your
ANIMAL (PLURAL)

friends.

MAD LIBS® is fun to play with friends, but you can also play it by yourself! To begin with, DO NOT look at the story on the page below. Fill in the blanks on this page with the words called for. Then, using the words you have selected, fill in the blank spaces in the story.

Now you've created your own hilarious MAD LIBS® game!

I NEED A NEW LAB PARTNER!

PERSON IN ROOM (MALE) _____

ADJECTIVE _____

LAST NAME _____

PERSON IN ROOM (FEMALE) _____

ADJECTIVE _____

VERB (PAST TENSE) _____

NOUN _____

ADJECTIVE _____

NOUN _____

ADJECTIVE _____

ADJECTIVE _____

PLURAL NOUN _____

ADJECTIVE _____

MAD LIBS®
I NEED A NEW LAB PARTNER!

To Whom It May Concern:

Hi. My name is _____ , and I am looking for a new,
                PERSON IN ROOM (MALE)

_____ lab partner for Mrs. _____'s biology class.
   ADJECTIVE   LAST NAME

My last lab partner, _____ , was really
                     PERSON IN ROOM (FEMALE)

_____ and never _____ our experiments
   ADJECTIVE   VERB (PAST TENSE)

on time. So I asked to switch, and the teacher said if I wanted

another _____ partner, I had to find one all by myself. If
          NOUN

you are smart, _____ in school, and always turn your
                 ADJECTIVE

_____-work in on time, you'd be a/an _____ lab
    NOUN   ADJECTIVE

partner for me. Please only contact me if you're _____
                                                   ADJECTIVE

about science and love doing scientific _____ . If this
                                          PLURAL NOUN

describes you, contact me at scienceluvr1@-_____-mail.
                                             ADJECTIVE

com, or just find me by my locker after lunch.

From MAD SCIENTIST MAD LIBS® • Copyright © 2014 by Price Stern Sloan,
an imprint of Penguin Group (USA) LLC, 345 Hudson Street, New York, NY 10014.

MAD LIBS® is fun to play with friends, but you can also play it by yourself! To begin with, DO NOT look at the story on the page below. Fill in the blanks on this page with the words called for. Then, using the words you have selected, fill in the blank spaces in the story.

Now you've created your own hilarious MAD LIBS® game!

MY WACKY
CHEMISTRY TEACHER

LAST NAME _____

PART OF THE BODY (PLURAL) _____

NOUN _____

EXCLAMATION _____

PERSON IN ROOM (FEMALE) _____

ADVERB _____

NOUN _____

ADJECTIVE _____

NOUN _____

EXCLAMATION _____

VERB (PAST TENSE) _____

NOUN _____

ADJECTIVE _____

MAD⊙LIBS®
MY WACKY
CHEMISTRY TEACHER

There are a lot of rumors going around about Mr. _Pike_ ,
LAST NAME

our chemistry teacher. He always has a crazy look in his

ears . Sometimes, in the middle of a/an
PART OF THE BODY (PLURAL)

cars lesson, he'll shout "_wow_!" for no reason at
NOUN   EXCLAMATION

all. My friend _Celeste_ told me that he acts
PERSON IN ROOM (FEMALE)

quietly because one time during a/an _line_-storm
ADVERB   NOUN

he was struck by lightning in his classroom. Ouch! That would

probably explain why he is so _spotty_ all the time and shakes
ADJECTIVE

whenever he writes on the _glass_-board. Last week, while
NOUN

doing an experiment in class, he yelled, "_Yes_! It's alive!"
EXCLAMATION

and then _Jumped_ around the room holding a/an
VERB (PAST TENSE)

Hat full of mysterious bubbling liquid. Maybe the rumors
NOUN

are true; maybe my teacher really is _black_!
ADJECTIVE

MAD LIBS® is fun to play with friends, but you can also play it by yourself! To begin with, DO NOT look at the story on the page below. Fill in the blanks on this page with the words called for. Then, using the words you have selected, fill in the blank spaces in the story.

Now you've created your own hilarious MAD LIBS® game!

AT-HOME EXPERIMENT #1: FLOATING PAPER CLIPS!

NUMBER _____

ADJECTIVE _____

ADJECTIVE _____

TYPE OF LIQUID _____

ADJECTIVE _____

ADVERB _____

NOUN _____

VERB ENDING IN "S" _____

VERB _____

PART OF THE BODY (PLURAL) _____

MAD⊙LIBS®
AT-HOME EXPERIMENT #1: FLOATING PAPER CLIPS!

Materials:

___10,000___ paper clips
NUMBER

A piece of ___crazy___ paper
ADJECTIVE

A see-through ___weird___-size bowl
ADJECTIVE

A pencil

Instructions:

1. Fill the bowl with ___Pepsi___.
   TYPE OF LIQUID

2. Rip a/an ___flowery___ piece of tissue paper and ___akva [?]___
   ADJECTIVE   ADVERB

   drop it onto the water.

3. Drop one of the ___zebra___ clips onto the tissue paper.
   NOUN

4. Use the pencil to gently nudge the tissue paper until the paper

   clip ___jumps___.
   VERB ENDING IN "S"

5. If you do this just right, the paper clip will start to ___jump___
   VERB

   in front of your very ___forearms___!
   PART OF THE BODY (PLURAL)

MAD LIBS® is fun to play with friends, but you can also play it by yourself! To begin with, DO NOT look at the story on the page below. Fill in the blanks on this page with the words called for. Then, using the words you have selected, fill in the blank spaces in the story.

Now you've created your own hilarious MAD LIBS® game!

FAMOUS SCIENTISTS

PLURAL NOUN _____

ADJECTIVE _____

NOUN _____

ADJECTIVE _____

VERB _____

NOUN _____

ADJECTIVE _____

SILLY WORD _____

PLURAL NOUN _____

ADJECTIVE _____

VERB (PAST TENSE) _____

ADVERB _____

ANIMAL _____

PLURAL NOUN _____

MAD LIBS

FAMOUS SCIENTISTS

Over the years, many famous _elephents_ have developed
_____PLURAL NOUN_____

beautiful theories, inventions, and ideas that have contributed to
___ADJECTIVE___

the evolution of _street_-kind. Below are some of the most
_____NOUN_____

come scientists to ever _jump_.
__ADJECTIVE__   __VERB__

Galileo Galilei was an Italian _bathroom_ who invented telescopes
_____NOUN_____

and found out a lot of information about the _Crazy_ Way
_____ADJECTIVE_____

Galaxy, the solar system, and planets like Jupiter and _Blala-Blab_
_____SILLY WORD_____

Sir Isaac Newton discovered most of what we now know about gravity.

He also wrote scientific _Cars_ called the First Law of
_____PLURAL NOUN_____

Motion, the Second Law of Motion, and the _weird_ Law of
_____ADJECTIVE_____

Motion.

Charles Darwin invented theories about natural selection, which

proved how different species _stalked_ over hundreds of
_____VERB (PAST TENSE)_____

years on Earth. He _Suprizingly_ studied several species of
_____ADVERB_____

zebra on the Galapagos _Seas_.
__ANIMAL__   __PLURAL NOUN__

MAD LIBS® is fun to play with friends, but you can also play it by yourself! To begin with, DO NOT look at the story on the page below. Fill in the blanks on this page with the words called for. Then, using the words you have selected, fill in the blank spaces in the story.

Now you've created your own hilarious MAD LIBS® game!

TURN YOUR BEDROOM INTO A SECRET LAB

ADJECTIVE _____

ADJECTIVE _____

VERB ENDING IN "ING" _____

NOUN _____

VERB _____

PLURAL NOUN _____

NOUN _____

ADJECTIVE _____

TYPE OF CONTAINER (PLURAL) _____

TYPE OF LIQUID _____

ADVERB _____

ADJECTIVE _____

VERB ENDING IN "ING" _____

MAD LIBS
TURN YOUR BEDROOM
INTO A SECRET LAB

Follow these _____ steps to turn your boring, _____

ADJECTIVE   ADJECTIVE

bedroom into a fully _____ science lab! First, put a big

VERB ENDING IN "ING"

_____ on your bedroom door that reads KEEP OUT! Scientists

NOUN

need to _____ in silence without any annoying

VERB

_____ interrupting them. Then clear off your

PLURAL NOUN

_____. You'll need it to hold all your oozy, _____

NOUN   ADJECTIVE

chemicals. Gather a bunch of _____ and put them

TYPE OF CONTAINER (PLURAL)

all over your desk. Connect them with tubing so you can watch all the

_____ run through them—_____ cool! Finally,

TYPE OF LIQUID   ADVERB

pull your curtains shut—you don't want anyone to see what kind of

_____ concoctions you're _____!

ADJECTIVE   VERB ENDING IN "ING"

MAD LIBS® is fun to play with friends, but you can also play it by yourself! To begin with, DO NOT look at the story on the page below. Fill in the blanks on this page with the words called for. Then, using the words you have selected, fill in the blank spaces in the story.

Now you've created your own hilarious MAD LIBS® game!

THE MAD SCIENTIST'S SHOPPING LIST

PLURAL NOUN _____

PART OF THE BODY _____

ARTICLE OF CLOTHING _____

VERB ENDING IN "ING" _____

ANIMAL (PLURAL) _____

PLURAL NOUN _____

NOUN _____

ADJECTIVE _____

VERB _____

NOUN _____

MAD LIBS
THE MAD SCIENTIST'S
SHOPPING LIST

- Long, rubbery black _____ to wear on your
  PLURAL NOUN

  hands

- Giant round _____-glasses with black frames
  PART OF THE BODY

- Long white lab _____
  ARTICLE OF CLOTHING

- Two beakers—one to hold in each hand while

  _____ maniacally
  VERB ENDING IN "ING"

- Several cages for all your lab _____
  ANIMAL (PLURAL)

- Assorted _____ floating in formaldehyde to add
  PLURAL NOUN

  to your collection

- A chalkboard and a piece of _____ to write down
  NOUN

  your _____ hypotheses and equations
  ADJECTIVE

- A giant electrical power switch to turn on when you need to

  _____ something to life
  VERB

- A Bunsen burner to light every _____ on fire!
  NOUN

MAD LIBS® is fun to play with friends, but you can also play it by yourself! To begin with, DO NOT look at the story on the page below. Fill in the blanks on this page with the words called for. Then, using the words you have selected, fill in the blank spaces in the story.

Now you've created your own hilarious MAD LIBS® game!

MORE FAMOUS SCIENTISTS

ADJECTIVE _____

ADJECTIVE _____

NOUN _____

PLURAL NOUN _____

PERSON IN ROOM (MALE) _____

OCCUPATION _____

NOUN _____

VERB _____

NOUN _____

PLURAL NOUN _____

COLOR _____

NOUN _____

MAD LIBS
MORE FAMOUS SCIENTISTS

Here are a few more _____ scientists!
                        ADJECTIVE

Nikola Tesla was born in Croatia. Later, he moved to the

_____ States of America and became an inventor. He helped
   ADJECTIVE

create fluorescent _____-bulbs so that people wouldn't have
                        NOUN

to use _____ to light their homes. Tesla also invented radio
        PLURAL NOUN

and worked with _____ Edison to invent things that
                  PERSON IN ROOM (MALE)

helped electricity work.

Alexander Graham Bell was a/an _____ from the nineteenth
                                    OCCUPATION

century. His mother was deaf, as was his _____. Because of
                                            NOUN

this, Bell was interested in speech and hearing. He decided to create

something that would help people _____ each other, no
                                    VERB

matter where they were. He invented the tele-_____ so that
                                                NOUN

people could talk to one another.

Stephen Hawking is a British physicist who studies galaxies and solar

_____. He has discovered a lot about _____ holes.
 PLURAL NOUN   COLOR

His most famous book is called *A Brief History of* _____.
                                                       NOUN

From MAD SCIENTIST MAD LIBS® • Copyright © 2014 by Price Stern Sloan,
an imprint of Penguin Group (USA) LLC, 345 Hudson Street, New York, NY 10014.

MAD LIBS® is fun to play with friends, but you can also play it by yourself! To begin with, DO NOT look at the story on the page below. Fill in the blanks on this page with the words called for. Then, using the words you have selected, fill in the blank spaces in the story.

Now you've created your own hilarious MAD LIBS® game!

FRANKENSTEIN'S MONSTER

NUMBER _____

NOUN _____

ADJECTIVE _____

COLOR _____

NOUN _____

PLURAL NOUN _____

PART OF THE BODY _____

PART OF THE BODY _____

ADJECTIVE _____

VERB (PAST TENSE) _____

ARTICLE OF CLOTHING _____

ADJECTIVE _____

ADJECTIVE _____

NOUN _____

MAD LIBS

FRANKENSTEIN'S MONSTER

Frankenstein's monster was a hideous, _____-foot-tall

NUMBER

_____. His skin was a/an _____ shade of

NOUN   ADJECTIVE

_____, his head was shaped like a/an _____, and he

COLOR   NOUN

had _____ sticking out of both sides of his neck.

PLURAL NOUN

Frankenstein's monster also had black lips and spiky black hair on his

_____, and his _____ was filled with big white

PART OF THE BODY   PART OF THE BODY

teeth. His _____ arms stuck straight out whenever he

ADJECTIVE

_____ down the street, because the black shirt and

VERB (PAST TENSE)

_____ he always wore were too small on his

ARTICLE OF CLOTHING

grotesque, _____ body. What a/an _____-looking

ADJECTIVE   ADJECTIVE

_____ he was!

NOUN

MAD LIBS® is fun to play with friends, but you can also play it by yourself! To begin with, DO NOT look at the story on the page below. Fill in the blanks on this page with the words called for. Then, using the words you have selected, fill in the blank spaces in the story.

Now you've created your own hilarious MAD LIBS® game!

AT-HOME EXPERIMENT #2: ERUPTING VOLCANO!

NOUN _____

ADJECTIVE _____

COLOR _____

VERB ENDING IN "ING" _____

TYPE OF LIQUID _____

ADJECTIVE _____

NOUN _____

PLURAL NOUN _____

ADJECTIVE _____

NUMBER _____

VERB _____

MAD LIBS
AT-HOME EXPERIMENT #2:
ERUPTING VOLCANO!

Materials:

A homemade volcano made out of plaster or ___dog food___-mâché

NOUN

A small ___sloay___ container

ADJECTIVE

___Brown___ or yellow food coloring

COLOR

___fxing___ soda

VERB ENDING IN "ING"

___molasses___

TYPE OF LIQUID

Dish soap

Instructions:

1. Put the ___discusting___ container at the top of your volcano.

ADJECTIVE

2. Pour in a little bit of baking soda and some dish
   ___rock___.

NOUN

3. Add a few ___furfignuggens___ of ___tasty___ food

PLURAL NOUN   ADJECTIVE
   coloring.

4. Pour in ___4.7___ ounces of vinegar.

NUMBER

5. Watch your volcano ___run___ with lava!

VERB

MAD LIBS® is fun to play with friends, but you can also play it by yourself! To begin with, DO NOT look at the story on the page below. Fill in the blanks on this page with the words called for. Then, using the words you have selected, fill in the blank spaces in the story.

Now you've created your own hilarious MAD LIBS® game!

THE WORST SCI-FI NIGHTMARE I EVER HAD

OCCUPATION _____

PART OF THE BODY _____

ADJECTIVE _____

PLURAL NOUN _____

VERB _____

ADJECTIVE _____

NOUN _____

PART OF THE BODY (PLURAL) _____

VERB _____

COLOR _____

TYPE OF LIQUID _____

NOUN _____

ADJECTIVE _____

MAD LIBS®
THE WORST SCI-FI
NIGHTMARE I EVER HAD

I had a dream last night that a crazy _____ was trying to
                                          OCCUPATION

perform experiments on me. He took a strand of my _____
                                                    PART OF THE BODY

and looked at it under a microscope. Then he told me to sit in his

_____chair. But I was scared—there were a bunch of electrical
ADJECTIVE

_____ tied to it, and I was afraid he was going to
PLURAL NOUN

_____ me in it! I said, "No, thanks, you _____
VERB   ADJECTIVE

scientist—I'm getting the _____ out of here." He looked me
                              NOUN

right in the _____ and said, "Don't you dare try to
              PART OF THE BODY (PLURAL)

leave my dungeon! You can't _____—the door's locked!"
                              VERB

Suddenly, he pounced on me, and everything turned to

_____. I woke up with _____ running down my
COLOR   TYPE OF LIQUID

temples. Thank _____ that nightmare is over. I hope I never
                  NOUN

see that _____scientist ever again!
          ADJECTIVE

MAD LIBS® is fun to play with friends, but you can also play it by yourself! To begin with, DO NOT look at the story on the page below. Fill in the blanks on this page with the words called for. Then, using the words you have selected, fill in the blank spaces in the story.

Now you've created your own hilarious MAD LIBS® game!

AT-HOME EXPERIMENT #3: TORNADO IN A BOTTLE!

NOUN _____

VERB ENDING IN "ING" _____

VERB _____

ADJECTIVE _____

ADJECTIVE _____

VERB _____

NOUN _____

NOUN _____

ADJECTIVE _____

NOUN _____

ADJECTIVE _____

VERB (PAST TENSE) _____

MAD LIBS®
AT-HOME EXPERIMENT #3: TORNADO IN A BOTTLE!

Materials:

Water

A see-through plastic soda _____ with a cap
                               NOUN

Glitter, to see debris _____ in the bottle
                        VERB ENDING IN "ING"

Dish soap to make your tornado _____
                                     VERB

Instructions:

1. Fill the entire _____ bottle with water until it is
                      ADJECTIVE

   almost all the way _____.
                          ADJECTIVE

2. _____ a few drops of dish _____ into the
        VERB   NOUN

   bottle. Add the _____ glitter.
                      ADJECTIVE

3. Screw the _____ onto the top of the bottle.
                 NOUN

4. Turn the bottle upside_____ and hold it near the cap.
                          ADJECTIVE

5. Spin the bottle in a/an _____-wise rotation.
                              NOUN

6. Stop spinning the bottle and admire the _____
                                               ADJECTIVE

   tornado you _____!
                 VERB (PAST TENSE)

MAD LIBS® is fun to play with friends, but you can also play it by yourself! To begin with, DO NOT look at the story on the page below. Fill in the blanks on this page with the words called for. Then, using the words you have selected, fill in the blank spaces in the story.

Now you've created your own hilarious MAD LIBS® game!

THE FIRST WEEK OF SCIENCE CLASS

ADJECTIVE _____

LAST NAME _____

PLURAL NOUN _____

PLURAL NOUN _____

NOUN _____

NOUN _____

ANIMAL (PLURAL) _____

PERSON IN ROOM _____

ADJECTIVE _____

VERB _____

THE FIRST WEEK OF SCIENCE CLASS

My first few days of science class were so _____! Our teacher,
ADJECTIVE

Miss _____, taught us all about matter and energy, atoms
LAST NAME

and _____, and the difference between solids, _____,
PLURAL NOUN   PLURAL NOUN

and gases. We even got to watch a video about gravity and why things

in outer _____ float but things on Earth fall to the
NOUN

_____! Our teacher says that next week we're going to do our
NOUN

first experiment and that, if we want, some day this year we can even

dissect _____! My friend _____ thought
ANIMAL (PLURAL)   PERSON IN ROOM

dissecting sounded gross, but I think it sounds really _____! I
ADJECTIVE

can't wait to _____ more about science next week.
VERB

From MAD SCIENTIST MAD LIBS® • Copyright © 2014 by Price Stern Sloan,
an imprint of Penguin Group (USA) LLC, 345 Hudson Street, New York, NY 10014.

This book is published by

PSS!

PRICE STERN SLOAN

whose other splendid titles include
such literary classics as

Ad Lib Mad Libs®
All I Want for Christmas Is Mad Libs®
Best of Mad Libs®
Camp Daze Mad Libs®
Christmas Carol Mad Libs®
Christmas Fun Mad Libs®
Cool Mad Libs®
Dance Mania Mad Libs®
Dear Valentine Letters Mad Libs®
Diva Girl Mad Libs®
Dude, Where's My Mad Libs®
Easter Eggstravaganza Mad Libs®
Escape from Detention Mad Libs®
Family Tree Mad Libs®
Girls Just Wanna Have Mad Libs®
Gobble Gobble Mad Libs®
Goofy Mad Libs®
Grab Bag Mad Libs®
Graduation Mad Libs®
Grand Slam Mad Libs®
Hanukkah Mad Libs®
Happily Ever Mad Libs®
Happy Birthday Mad Libs®
Haunted Mad Libs®
Holly, Jolly Mad Libs®
Hot Off the Presses Mad Libs®
Kid Libs Mad Libs®
Letters from Camp Mad Libs®
Luck of the Mad Libs®

Mad About Mad Libs®
Mad About Animals Mad Libs®
Mad Libs® for President
Mad Libs® Forever
Mad Libs® from Outer Space
Mad Libs® in Love
Mad Libs® on the Road
Mad Mad Mad Mad Mad Libs®
Mad Scientist Mad Libs®
Monster Mad Libs®
More Best of Mad Libs®
Night of the Living Mad Libs®
Ninjas Mad Libs®
Off-the-Wall Mad Libs®
The Original #1 Mad Libs®
P. S. I Love Mad Libs®
Peace, Love, and Mad Libs®
Pirates Mad Libs®
Rock 'n' Roll Mad Libs®
Slam Dunk Mad Libs®
Sleepover Party Mad Libs®
Sooper Dooper Mad Libs®
Spooky Mad Libs®
Straight "A" Mad Libs®
Totally Pink Mad Libs®
Undead Mad Libs®
Vacation Fun Mad Libs®
Winter Games Mad Libs®
You've Got Mad Libs®

and many, many more!
Mad Libs® are available wherever books are sold.